ARUNDEL
Past & Present

A Pictorial Guide

NICHOLAS THORNTON

Ensign
PUBLICATIONS

Published by **Ensign Publications**
A division of Hampshire Books Ltd.,
2 Redcar Street, Southampton SO1 5LL

Designed and typeset by
PageMerger, Southampton

Edited by David Graves

British Library Cataloguing in Publication Data
Thornton, Nicholas
 Arundel past and present: a pictorial guide.
 1. West Sussex. Arundel, history
 I. Title
 942.2'67

ISBN 185455 010 1

Dedication

To Wendy and Philip

ACKNOWLEDGEMENTS

Many thanks to the following for their help with this book. My mother and father, Peter Akhurst, Wilfred Herington, Tom Hendrick, Neil Holland, The Convent of Poor Clares, Crossbush. Mr Puttock, Castle Comptroller, and his deputy Mr Peachy and other staff. The proprietor of the Swan Hotel, British Gas, John Godfrey, Oliver Hawkins, Roger Halls, Martin Hayes and others at the local studies library, Worthing. Miss Northeast, Joss Davis, G.H. Lee, W.E.J. Bishop, Arthur King, John Taft, Arundel Tourist Information Centre. Other Arundel residents whose names I never learnt.

INTRODUCTION

Arundel has developed continuously from the Norman Conquest to 1900. Since then the town has changed hardly at all. As a result, the Victorian buildings which line its streets are interspersed with ones from various prior ages.

Flint and earthworks prove that the site was occupied in prehistory. The remains of a villa under Tarrant Street and coins and artifacts found at various places, prove that it was occupied in Roman times. The later inhabitants were probably a friendly British tribe who held the strategic position for their colonial masters.

The Saxons too had a small village there. King Alfred may have had a fort at Arundel, but this is not certain.

After the Norman Conquest western Sussex found itself lying across a principal route between the new King William and his Dukedom of Normandy. He therefore gave it to one of his most trusted supporters, Roger de Montgomery, making him Earl of Arundel.

Here Roger built himself a wooden castle. He chose the site because it stood on a hill protected on three sides by water. It also commanded good views of the coast and the Arun valley, and enjoyed good river communication with the Channel.

Despite much alteration, Roger's castle retains its Norman structure – a mound topped by a keep, with an adjoining wall enclosing a courtyard. Soon afterwards, he added its stone gateway.

This castle was strong enough to withstand its first siege. In 1102 the third Earl, Robert de Belleme, rebelled against

Henry I. After three fruitless months Henry left his siege equipment at Arundel to deal with Robert at his main castle at Bridgenorth. Henry exiled Robert and stripped him of his title.

In 1138 William de Albini, a Norman from Norfolk, became the fourth earl. The keep in which he and his retainers lived he rebuilt in stone. It is probable that he rebuilt other parts in stone also.

In the following year, Henry I's nephew Stephen and daughter Matilda were fighting for the throne. Matilda arrived at Arundel from the continent and Stephen laid siege to her in the castle. Stephen however soon lifted the siege and agreed to allow Matilda to join her supporters in Bristol. (Eventually they agreed that Stephen should reign and that Matilda's son should succeed him. The later became Henry II.)

After Henry II's accession, Earl William gave him the castle. Henry rebuilt more of it in stone. The Well Tower, attached to the keep, and Bevis's Tower to the north are of this period, and may be his work. Other parts, such as the east wing and the square tower to the north, were also built in stone at this time.

Henry then handed it back to the earls. The ninth, Richard Fitzalan, made more improvements at the end of the thirteenth century. These included the Barbican Towers which he placed in front of Roger's gateway. Thus by about 1300 the castle was built entirely of stone.

When the 20th Earl, Henry Fitzalan, died in 1580 the estate passed to his daughter Mary. She married Thomas Howard, the fourth Duke of Norfolk, thereby uniting the two titles.

The castle saw much action during the Civil War. Parliament realised that by retaining Sussex's strongest castle, the Royalists would be able to keep in touch with their friends on the continent. In 1642 the Duke was absent and it was garrisoned by just 100 men. The Roundheads therefore sent a small force under General Sir William Waller which captured it in December. Royalist General Hopton however, retook it twelve months later. He left over 1,000 men behind to defend the town and the castle.

Parliament immediately sent General Waller with 10,000 men to retake it. His troops soon evicted the defenders from their hastily dug entrenchments to the north of the town. The Royalists retreated into the castle, fighting as they did so. Sir William bombarded the castle from the Maison Dieu, the tower of St Nicholas', and emplacements in the park. The marks made by his cannon balls may still be seen on the Barbican. They drained Swanbourne Lake which caused the castle well to become contaminated. As a result the garrison surrendered in January 1644, three weeks after Waller's arrival.

Parliament garrisoned the castle until 1649. As they left, they knocked much of it down so as to render it useless to their enemies.

At the Restoration in 1660 the castle was returned to the Howards, but they preferred to live at their Norfolk estates and the castle remained in ruins. In 1716 the eighth Duke decided to return. He therefore repaired the castle and remodelled the south wing.

In 1791 Charles, the 11th Duke embarked upon an ambitious scheme of rebuilding. He designed what he believed the medieval castle had looked like.

He started on the south-east tower and the south wing. Work began upon the east wing in 1801 and the west wing in

1806. The whole was a romanticised view of the past and full of allusions to the liberties of Magna Carta.

He also acquired much land to the north of his castle-home to form Arundel Park. He filled it with deer, planted trees, and extended Swanbourne Lake. In 1807 he diverted London Road so that it ran to the south of St Nicholas' Church, and thence along the western edge of the new park.

The 12th Duke acquired more land thereby doubling the size of the park. He and the 13th Duke made other improvements to the grounds described more fully below.

In 1892 Henry the 15th Duke completed the acquisition of land surrounding the castle. Moreover, he felt that his predecessor's ornate building was not what a medieval castle really looked like, and that the materials and execution were poor.

Between 1874 and 1907 therefore he had much of Charles' work torn down and replaced with a more faithful reproduction designed by Charles Buckler. It was executed to the highest standards using only the finest materials. Work on the kitchen block and private apartments were begun in 1879, and the structure, including a new west wing was completed by 1894. Refurnishing continued until 1901.

The final phase, restoration of the keep and Bevis's Tower, was completed in 1907. Henry's "medieval" castle was fitted with contemporary conveniences such as central heating and electric light. Today's building is principally that of the 15th Duke. The library, with its rich carvings, is one of the few of Charles' works that has been retained.

The arrival of Earl Roger and the Normans and the buildings of the castle gave a great boost to the village outside its walls. It expanded and within a few years was made a borough with a mayor and burgesses.

Its liberties helped the town to prosper commercially from this time. This cushioned the fortunes of its inhabitants during most of the ups and downs of the noble residents of the castle.

Two centuries later Arundel was still small. Farming and fishing were its most important occupations and the river provided an important link for cross-Channel trade.

In 1295 the ninth Earl, Richard Fitzalan, built a wall westwards from the castle around the north and west sides of the town. It was pierced by two gates. What is now Maltravers Street ended in the Water Gate. The London Road left the town via St Mary's Gate in the north wall.

By the beginning of the fifteenth century the basic plan of today's Arundel had been laid down. Its craftsmen, traders, and small farmer-citizens lived in timber-framed houses with thatched roofs. The port was developing and the river was an important route for trade and transport.

Elizabeth I confirmed the borough's privileges in her charter of 1586. These included the right to hold markets every week and fairs three times per year. Trade included cattle, sheep, timber, salt and corn. The position was again confirmed by Charles II in 1677. (The borough was finally dissolved on 31st March 1974 as part of the local government reorganisation.)

Sir William Waller's Parliamentary forces had damaged the town considerably, including burning and knocking down some houses in the town and desecrating the Fitzalan Chapel. Fearing for their lives, many of the townspeople had fled during the fighting. During their absence, much of their property was looted. When order was restored in the town its citizens claimed large sums in compensation which were met in full by Parliament.

Despite the absence of the Dukes, Arundel continued to hold markets for agricultural produce from a wide hinterland. These were held in Lower Market (now Maltravers) Street. They were later moved to Market Square in High Street, where cattle continued to be sold until 1898.

Around 1800 Arundel was a fashionable rendezvous for the nobility and gentry. In addition, many young officers waiting to serve in the French wars congregated there. It had its own winter season whose social activities rivalled nearby Brighton.

These included theatre-going. Plays were being performed from 1792 in the yard of the Angel Inn. In 1807 a Mr Thornton converted a malthouse in Maltravers Street into a theatre. It closed in 1833 because its small income prevented it from engaging the acts and performers that the public came to expect, and which theatres in Worthing and Brighton were able to provide.

This period saw the height of the town's prosperity. The population increased from 2188 in 1811 to 2803 in 1831. More houses were built particularly in Tarrant Street and Maltravers Street. Several of its sixteenth-century timber-framed buildings were given brick or stucco facades and doors under fanlights or pediments. The former Crown Inn in High Street is a good example of this.

The Dukes of Norfolk were the landlords of large numbers of houses in Arundel. Besides the castle, the 11th-15th Dukes also wanted to remodel the town as they believed it may have looked like in the Middle Ages.

The mock-tudor post office at the bottom of High Street is an example of this. There are many others in High Street and Maltravers Street. In London Road the castle's electricity generating station was built in a mock-medieval style. Indeed it is so much a feature of Arundel, that a house has been constructed in Parson's Hill in a similar style.

Also of this spirit and period is the neo-Norman Town Hall in Maltravers Street and the Home Farm buildings north of the castle. The rear of the Maltravers Street theatre, visible from the castle grounds, was finished in a Gothic style to conform with the Duke's taste.

Arundel's strong religious connections began with the Norman Conquest. It was an expression of the Earls' concern for the well-being of their souls in the next world. Roger de Montgomery founded a priory which adjoined St Nicholas'. Adeliza, wife of William de Albini, founded the Priory of Calceto. Its remains are today incorporated into Priory Farm, next to the railway station.

There has been a church on the site of St Nicholas for many centuries – perhaps since Saxon times. The 12th Earl, Richard Fitzalan, had it entirely rebuilt in 1380. He replaced Roger's priory with an ecclesiastical college built around a quadrangle with cloisters. It housed a community of priests and lay members.

These priests held their services in the chancel of St Nicholas, which was separated from the rest of the church by an iron grille. The college was suppressed by Henry VIII who sold it and the chancel to Henry, the 20th Earl.

For the next 200 years services were held in the nave whilst the college and blocked-off chancel were unused. The 11th Duke converted the ruined college into a Catholic chapel for public worship, and a house for the priest. The 12th Duke re-acquired the Fitzalan Chapel which the borough council were using for meetings.

Today the church is much as it was in 1380. One half is used for Anglican services, and the other half, the Fitzalan Chapel, for Catholic worship by the Duke of Norfolk's family.

In the nineteenth century the college was rebuilt as a Catholic chapel and house for the estate manager. Today it is run as sheltered accommodation.

Earl Richard also founded in 1396 the Maison Dieu, whose remains stand on the north bank of the Arun by the bridge. It was an almshouse for poor men who could recite certain prayers in Latin. There they lived a semi-monastic life. It too was dissolved in the Reformation.

In 1873 St Philip Neri, also in London Road, was built under the Duke's patronage as the town's Catholic church. Since 1829 Catholics had been achieving emancipation, and its ambitious scale represents their increasing self-confidence. It was modelled on Gothic churches in France.

The church's architect Hansom (designer of the Hansom Cab) intended to complete it with a tall steeple, and a base for it was built. However he realised that the weight of the structure might cause the whole to slip downhill. The building was therefore finished off with a small steeple or "fleche" rising from the centre of the roof.

In 1965 it became the cathedral of the Arundel and Brighton diocese and was re-dedicated to St Philip Howard, the 21st Earl. St Philip died in 1595 whilst imprisoned for his Catholic faith by Queen Elizabeth (who had deprived him of the Dukedom).

The port of Arundel was deep enough to take early medieval ships. During Earl Roger's time they may have unloaded their cargoes below the town at Ford. Their passage however was impeded by the sand bar which the sea continually deposited across the river's mouth. From time to time the Earls helped the port by having it dredged.

In 1560 Henry, the 20th Earl, improved the harbour at Arundel so that large vessels could tie up at the present town quay. This may have included an alteration in the river's course, or it may have been merely a deepening for large ships. In either event, the port expanded from this period.

During the sixteenth and seventeenth centuries large vessels continued to dock at Arundel, and trade grew in corn, bacon, salt, wine, timber, stone and metals. In addition, considerable quantities of fish were landed on the quayside.

One of the reasons for the continued prosperity of the port was its position on an inland waterway system formed during the Industrial Revolution. In the eighteenth century the mouth of the river at Littlehampton was improved and the reaches above Arundel were shortened and straightened to facilitate navigation.

Similar improvements to the Rother, a tributary which drains into the Arun above Arundel, were sponsored at the end of the century by Lord Egremont. He owned extensive farm estates in the Petworth area and these "navigations" facilitated transport for their corn, flour and timber.

Sailing barges brought these products to Arundel and Littlehampton. There they were transferred to sailing ships which exported them to the north of England, Ireland, France or Spain. At the same time coal shipped from north-east England and unloaded at Arundel was carried upriver in the barges.

Lord Egremont then turned his attention to connecting the Arun to the Wey, a navigable river which drained into the Thames. He enlisted the financial support of a group of his fellow peers, including the Duke of Norfolk. The Act of Parliament which gave the group the necessary powers was passed in 1813. The 20-mile Wey and Arun Canal was completed in 1816. Now there was an inland water route for barges from London to the south coast.

During the Napoleonic Wars military stores, personnel and pay was carried from London to Portsmouth. The government however, wished to avoid the sea route because of attacks by French raiders. Lord Egremont was the prime mover in the Arundel Canal, whose enabling act was passed in 1817 – after the war with France had ended. The canal was dug notwithstanding, joining Portsmouth to the Arun at Ford.

Arundel's importance as a port thus reached its height in the early 19th century. Docks were excavated in the south bank of the river, immediately to the west of the bridge. After about 1830 the port began to decline. Littlehampton gradually took over its trade and a few years later the growing railways, which transported goods more cheaply and quickly, hastened the process.

However, merchant ships of increasing size were bringing corn, coal, timber and salt to Arundel until the twentieth century. The railway crossed the river at Ford by a bridge whose central span could be rolled back for the tall-masted ships to pass.

During the 1935-7 however, electrification of the railway made such a bridge impractical. It was therefore replaced by a fixed bridge which prevented ships from reaching Arundel. Today the only traffic on the river are small pleasure-craft.

There has been a sawmill in Arundel on the river's north bank from Domesday to 1957. In the late sixteenth century warships, including perhaps those that fought in the Armada, were built there and it became known as the Nineveh Shipyard. Later the works reverted to a sawmill, where a wide variety of products were cut from English wood. Boat and fence timbers for example were made from oak, and cart-shafts and wheel parts from ash. Items were also sawn from beech, elm and sycamore.

During the Boer War, the sawmill cut large quantities of tent pegs for the troops in South Africa. In 1933 it began to import foreign timber and construct finished products. During the Second World War it made internal wooden fittings for motor torpedo boats. "Nineveh Shipyard" now makes metal goods.

Many of the old pictures on the following pages are paired with a photograph of the same view today. They illustrate some of the above points and other aspects of the town's past. I hope that they convey some of the richness and diversity of Arundel's history.

The Railway Station, c., 1930. Showing the railway before electrification. The far building on the right is the goods shed and opposite, the signal box. Behind each of these, sidings led off, including a branch into the former. Smoke on the left betrays the presence of a locomotive.

Quayside, c., 1890. The brig *Ebenezer* is discharging coal at the Co-operative Society's wharf. Every October such colliers used to fish off the coast of north-east England. There they sold their catch and returned to Sussex with coal. The buildings are warehouses; that in the picture's centre stored salt which was used by Arundel's grocers.

10

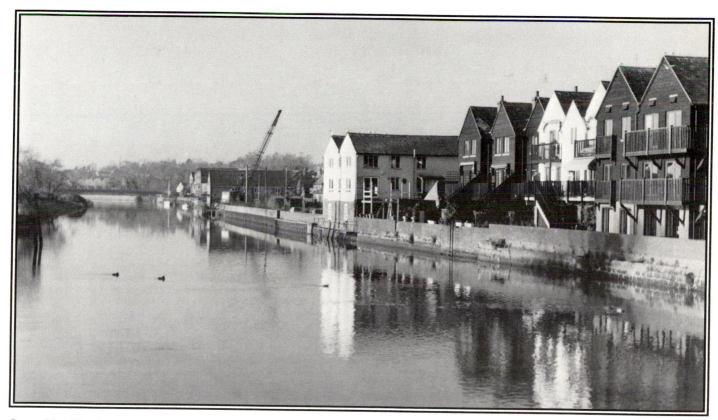

Quayside. The former salt warehouse is now Arundel Antiques Market. The buildings with the balconies in the foreground are modern flats built in a style similar to the former warehouse beside them. For this reason they won an Arundel Society award for development sympathetic to the character of the town.

The Bridge, 1900. There has been a bridge across the river on this site for many hundreds of years, perhaps since Domesday. During the twelfth century Queen Adeliza (the widow of Henry I) founded a priory to provide for the maintenance of a wooden bridge. A new one was built in 1507 which frequently needed repair. In 1724 it was replaced by the narrow stone bridge in the picture. In 1831 Mayor William Holmes widened it by adding cantilevered pavements with metal railings on their outer edges.

The Bridge. The present structure was built in 1935. People still go boating on the Arun for pleasure as they did in 1900. Just visible in the foreground are the jetties for privately-owned motor cruisers.

Arundel from Upriver, 1907. For many years after the coming of the railway, barges like this one continued to carry goods along the river. The large building in front of the cathedral is the Swallow Brewery. On its roof stood a 6-foot wooden statue of a swallow, the town symbol.

Arundel from Upriver. Today working barges have completely disappeared from the Arun. The Swallow Brewery was pulled down in the 1930s. The bird statue however was saved and remounted on the roof of the town hall in Maltravers Street.

ARUNDEL FROM THE RIVER

Arundel from Downriver, c., 1915. A collier is discharging coal at the gasworks. Most of this fuel came from north-east England. In 1821, at the peak of its prosperity as a port, 45 ships were registered at Arundel. Ships of up to 200 tons or more were towed up and down the narrow, fast-flowing river by the harbour tug, *Jumna*.

16

Arundel from Downriver. The commercial traffic to and from the port of Arundel finally ceased in the mid-1930s. This was caused by the construction of a fixed bridge across the river at Ford, two miles below the gasworks. The bridge in the middleground is part of the bypass, completed in October 1973.

Arundel Market 50 years ago

High Street, c., 1880. In 1773 a huddle of illegally-built houses at the foot of High Street were pulled down. The cleared area was named Market Square, to denote its new use. Specialising in fully-grown livestock, it was one of the most important in West Sussex. It finally closed in 1898 due to competition from others like that at Barnham.

High Street. Today the area in the foreground is used by U-turning motor vehicles. On certain holidays, side shows and the like are held there and in December a large Christmas tree is erected next to the war memorial.

The War Memorial and Environs, 1921. Paid for by a public subscription raised by the mayor, Wilfred Herington. The building in the extreme top right corner used to be Henty's Bank. The Henty's were an important local family who also brewed. A black horse was part of their coat of arms. It is said that Lloyd's Bank inherited it from them through various amalgamations.

War Memorial and Environs. The former Henty's Bank, now called Bank House, is divided into two. The three gables on the left all belong to the mock-Tudor post office built for the 15th Duke who was Postmaster-General. Larger than Arundel ever needed, today most of it is occupied by other businesses.

High Street, Arundel in 1828.

Top of High Street, 1828. "Dodger" Bartlett, whose shop is on the right, was an important local businessman. He traded in malt and hops and owned a flour mill, corn warehouse and coal yards on the town quay. The left edge of the picture is the corner of a fifteenth-century slaughterhouse.

Top of High Street. All the buildings of 1828 have now gone. Even the slaughterhouse was replaced in the 1880s by a mock-Tudor house. The latter was designed by Aloysius Hansom, who designed the Hansom Cab, and Arundel cathedral.

Quay at corner of High Street and River Road, 1930. The building on the right, originally a corn store, was later converted into a deck chair factory. The timber and canvas caught fire, and the town and Norfolk Estate fire brigades (pumping water from the Arun in the picture) were unable to prevent the building from being gutted.

Quay at corner of High Street and River Road. The site of the deck chair factory has been left an open space where anyone may sit and relax by the river. The building in the centre is Bank House. The finger-posts on the right are intended to guide tourists.

The Swan Inn c., 1870. One of the three oldest pubs in Arundel, it dates back to the fifteenth century and has always been called *The Swan*. In the foreground the proprietor's family, the Stevens, pose for their photograph. On the extreme left may be seen one of Arundel's gas lamps. Their pale flames lit its streets until 1969, when the town converted to electricity.

The Swan Inn today. The pub has been remodelled recently both inside and out. The work included extension northwards over the site of an adjoining shop, which was demolished. This is now the pub's dining room.

Tarrant Street, 1913. South side of its east end. The building in the background housed the drapers, Watts and Acott. An associated company, Watts and Nephew sold linen in the adjoining glass-fronted shop. The Arun was called the Tarrant from Roman times to the sixteenth century.

Tarrant Street. The buildings are structurally unchanged after three-quarters of a century. The businesses however are different. The former Watts and Nephew premises has been divided in two, and the shop-front in the centre of the picture has been reconstructed.

Former Pub, Tarrant Street, 1963. During the nineteenth century, there were a large number of pubs in Arundel, perhaps one for every 100 residents. Those at or near the quay had names such as *The Jolly Sailors* and *The Ship and Lighter*, and catered for the crews of vessels which called at the port.

Former Pub, Tarrant Street. For a time until the 1920s it was the *Queens Arms*. Like many former pubs in Arundel, it has been converted to a dwelling house and much modernised. Its structure dates back to the sixteenth century and one of its rooms was a chapel. Its cellars are Victorian and it has a well at the rear.

East end of Maltravers Street, 1908. In the seventeenth century the cottage on the left was the *Black Bull Inn*. It was severely damaged by the cannons of General Waller's Parliamentary army. In the 1890s some sixteenth-century cottages (on the extreme left) were demolished. This was to make way for a new road still called to this day "New Cut".

East end of Maltravers Street. Today it is entirely residential – witness the removal van. The only exception is the Town Hall whose tower rises above a roof on the right. When the borough was dissolved a town council with only a few powers was created and meets here occasionally. Arundel Magistrates' Court also sits here regularly.

Maltravers Street, 1907. Known as White Waistcoat Street, because it was where Arundel's business and professional class lived. In 1846 Queen Victoria and Prince Albert paid an official visit. Entering the town by Maltravers Street, their carriage got stuck in the snow as it came up the hill. For this reason the street was widened and a gentler gradient created.

Maltravers Street. Except for a lamp-post or two, nothing much has changed. Moreover it is still a well-to-do area of the town.

Castle Quadrangle, c., 1890. The last rebuilding by the fifteenth Duke replaced the ornate "Baronial" style with the more restrained "Early English Gothic". In the picture, the masons are rebuilding the South Wing. Throughout the work the architect paid the greatest attention to detail and used Caen stone from northern France, just as the Norman Earl Roger did.

Castle Quadrangle. Many of the rooms in this part of the castle are open to the public. The cars belong to the staff who are needed to clean and maintain the castle, even when it is closed or the Duke of Norfolk is absent.

Castle Keep, 1899. The eleventh Duke had left it a romantic ruin when he restored the remainder of his home a century previously. Within it he kept a group of large American owls as pets. These he waggishly named after individual politicians of the day; "Please Your Grace, Lord Thurlow has laid an egg," his butler once told him.

Castle Keep. The 15th Duke restored it shortly after the 1899 photograph was taken. Prominent in both is the square Well Tower, a thirteenth-century extension of the (circular) keep. Its well is 300 feet deep and supplied the keep with water. Today, a flag flying from the Well Tower indicates that the Duke is at the castle.

Castle Gateway, 1908. Charles the 11th Duke and his successors gradually acquired the land surrounding their castle-home. In 1833 for example the 12th Duke, Bernard, obtained and demolished houses on the east side of High Street. This made way for the gateway, designed by William Burn, and completed by the 13th Duke Henry Charles in 1851.

Castle Gateway, 1989. Modern cars and street signs contrast with the unchanged walls and gateway. The arms above the archway are those of the Fitzalan-Howard family, and the lion above it is an emblem of the Dukes of Norfolk. Visitors to the castle enter here in the spring, summer and autumn.

St. Philip Neri, Arundel.

Catholic Parish Church, 1913, when it was dedicated to an Italian saint, Philip Neri. The structure extending from its right is the base of the massive steeple that its architect Hansom designed but wisely decided not to complete. The low building on its immediate left is the presbytery where the priest lived.

Cathedral. The building's status was changed in 1965. The then Duke of Norfolk (Bernard Marmaduke, the sixteenth) used his influence to have it rededicated to his ancestor-saint, Philip Howard. In 1937 the castle converted the walled vegetable and fruit garden on the near side of London Road into a car park for visitors.

College House and Fitzalan Chapel, 1828. After the Reformation they were bought by the earls of Arundel, and much of the college was knocked down. The Roundheads desecrated the chapel's interior during the Civil War. The road is a stub of London Road which, after its diversion to the south of the college, the Duke of Norfolk finally enclosed in 1836. (Print from Rouse's Scraps of Sussex, 1828.)

College House and Fitzalan Chapel. Physically part of Arundel Church, ownership of the Fitzalan Chapel was disputed by the vicar. However in 1880 the High Court confirmed that it belonged to the Dukes of Norfolk. Soon afterwards they restored the buildings, taking great care to reproduce their former appearance.

St Nicholas' Church, 1829. One of the few British churches built in one style only – Perpendicular Gothic. At this time the interior walls and ceilings were plastered. The heavily overgrown building on the right was another part of the college. It belonged to the Dukes of Norfolk who in the anti-Catholic atmosphere prevalent at that time did not attempt to repair it.

St Nicholas' Church. The (broader) spire was completely renovated in 1860. Fourteen years later the architect Sir Gilbert Scott was commissioned to restore the church to its medieval appearance. He therefore had the eighteenth-century plaster stripped away, leaving it much as it is today.

Convent Schools, 1905 (another part of the old college attached to St Nicholas's). For about 50 years the schools were run by a community of nuns called the Servite Sisters. They left in about 1960 and moved their community to Bognor Regis. After that Mr and Mrs Eric St John-Foti used the school to look after children in care.

The Priory House. The block in the foreground is now "The Priory Playhouse", the theatre of The Arundel Players. The remainder is part of the sheltered accommodation run by the Knights of Malta. The latter received another of The Arundel Society's awards, for restoration of the roof of the Priory House.

Pumphouse and Cowshed, 1846. Designed by Robert Abraham for the 13th Duke in 1845. The nearer building pumped water to the castle. The other is the home farm's cowshed, and disappearing behind it is the old Mill Road. Those facades which were visible from the road, such as the pumphouse doorway, were finished in a neo-Norman style.

Former Pumphouse and Cowshed. The pumphouse has lost its roof and the motionless machinery inside is rusting. The cowshed is leased to The Wildfowl Trust who use it as a store for bird-feed. Still visible inside are drainage channels in the concrete floor and the sites of the cow-stalls.

Farmhouse and Dairy, c., 1907. Immediately south of the cowshed, also part of the Norfolk Estate's home farm. The model dairy (right) was lit by windows on seven of its eight sides and a roof lantern. Inside, the walls were tiled in blue and white, and a fountain kept the atmosphere clean and cool.

Former Farmhouse and Dairy. Today the farmhouse (left) is the home of the curator of The Wildfowl Trust Reserve – on the other side of the road. There the design of their modern pavilions was inspired by the dairy. They use the latter as a lumber room.

Swanbourne Lake, SE Corner c., 1922. The lake was the pond of a mill which had existed from Domesday until recently. Only since the formation of Arundel Park at the beginning of the nineteenth century, has Swanbourne been a place where the public may relax.

Swanbourne Lake, c., 1925. This view is just a little way up the north-east side of the lake. The silhouette of the castle can just be seen in the top right-hand corner. Today the shoreline has changed shape, and the recent gales have knocked down some of the trees on the left.

Bridge Street, c., 1916. *The White Hart* in the foreground was built at the end of the nineteenth century on the site of an old weather-boarded inn of the same name. The shop awnings are of A. Herington. Its drapery occupied the far gable of the White Hart building, and their outfitters the adjacent premises – Bridge House. Herington's remained on this site for 112 years.

Queen Street. The cottage with the two chimneys on the far corner of the bridge was Tom Buller's. The family hired out pleasure boats on the river for many generations. It was demolished in 1935. The street has been called Queen Street ever since the 1920s.

1 to 4 Queen Street, 1962. Arundel has many examples of the regional flint-and-brick architectural style. Flint is very hard-wearing and plentiful in the South Downs or on local beaches. The problem is that it will not make a strong corner, nor as a lintel will it support the wall above it. Consequently, these are made of brick, usually in gently contrasting red.

1 to 3 Queen Street. Number 4 was demolished after the left-hand photograph was taken. Masonry braces help strengthen the structure. The needless demolition of the end of the terrace has robbed Arundel of a well-proportioned building. The planners did not even specify that the chimney be re-created in its previous form.

The General Abercrombie, 1920. The proprietor's family pose for their photograph in the doorway. A Henty and Constable pub, it faced their Swallow Brewery across the road.

The General Abercrombie today. In 1936 the exterior and interior were modernised. The front was entirely rebuilt, and entrance is now via the passageway in its left corner. The wall of the old building can just be seen down the side on the right. Today the pub is a free house and popular with Arundel's young people.

Railway Station, 1904. Henry, the 15th Duke is just about to leave the station by carriage with his bride, Gwendolen Mary Constable Maxwell. She was his second wife, and was to become the mother of Bernard Marmaduke, the 16th Duke. Soldiers from the Yeomanry, with whom the Duke served in the Boer War, greet them.

Railway Station, 1989. The old London, Brighton and South Coast Railway buildings are today part of British Rail. The sidings where the carriages used to stand is now a car park for passengers.

The Black Rabbit, c., 1908. The public house is on the far side of the road almost hidden by the trees. It was frequented by navvies building the railway and altering the river. For the latter purpose blocks of chalk were carried by barges like the two in the picture.

The Black Rabbit, 1909. The public house was originally a terrace of cottages. (Contrast the opposite trend in the town.) Its patrons hired rowing skiffs from the publican – despite the fast current round the bend in the river.

Arundel from the ESE, 1846. This shows the castle as restored by Charles, the 11th Duke. The windmill in the centre of the picture stands in an area known as Portreeve's Acre. Built in 1769, it was one of several formerly at Arundel, and was demolished in 1864. There is little sign of flood walls along the riverbank.

Arundel from the ESE, 1989. The cathedral (1873), and the rebuilt castle have radically altered the skyline. The river is obscured by flood-walls, completed on the near bank early this century. The low building near the site of the mill is a cowshed, and in front runs the 1863 railway. Sheep and cattle however, still graze in the meadows.

Arundel from the SSE, 1798. At this time Charles was rebuilding the castle – notice the detached tower on the left. Beneath it The Causeway runs off to the right. The port was very active and the artist has included a sea-going ship in front of the warehouses on the quay.

Arundel from the SSE, 1989. Broadly similar after two centuries. The Causeway however has many more houses along it and the farm land has been enclosed. The motor vehicles in the middle distance are running along the 1973 bypass.

Ford Road, 1909. The gabled cottage half-way down on the right is a shop, as is the cottage on the extreme left. The structure at the end of the road is a gasometer. It is part of the gasworks at which the sailing ships unloaded coal as featured earlier in this book.

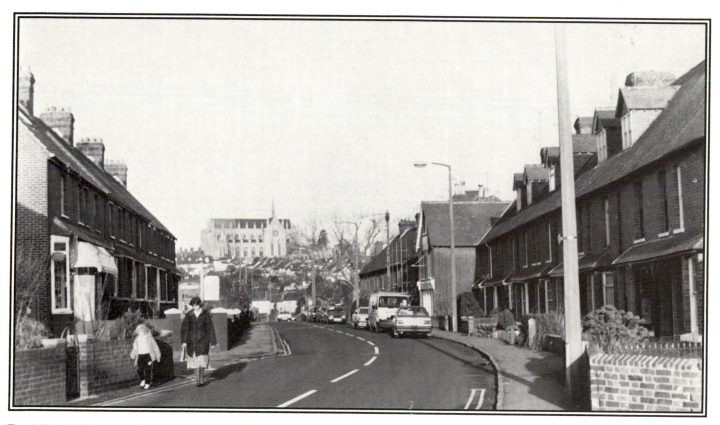

Ford Road. The scene is very similar today. The shop on the extreme left is still there; the shop on the right was there until recently, but is now the office of a local architect. The gas cylinder has gone but the area is still a British Gas pressure-reducing station.

Castle from the Meadow, c., 1910. The meadow was owned by the Duke of Norfolk who allowed children to play there. The Boats for Hire were rowing boats. In the late 1950s Bernard Marmaduke, the 16th Duke, gave the meadow to the town for the purpose of constructing a bathing pool.

Lower Marshes, c., 1900. The picture shows Gratwick Terrace shortly after it was built. It backs onto the east bank of the river just below the town. Despite its uniform appearance, the residents rented their cottages from various landlords.

Mary Gate, 1792 – by which London Road passed through the town walls. Probably at the time of erection, its top floor was made into the Chapel of Blessed Mary Over the Gate. There mass was celebrated daily until the Reformation. During the Civil War the top floor was knocked away completely. Here each side is roofed as a house.

74

Mary Gate today. At the beginning of the nineteenth century, Charles the 11th Duke expanded Arundel Park and diverted London Road. As a result, the gate found itself marooned in the castle grounds, and Charles restored it to its original appearance. Today the Arundel Festival Office use the room over the archway all the year round.

King's Arms Hill, 1963. Joining Maltravers and Tarrant Streets, it was named only recently, after the pub on its Tarrant Street corner. The picture shows that end of the King's Arms Hill, but the pub is just off to the right.

King's Arms Hill, 1989. Clearly the area has moved up-market in the last twenty-six years. The pictures show that this little corner of the town has undergone many improvements such as new windows, driveways and a garage extension.

Oasthouse, 1965. (Off Queen Street). Up to about 1900 it was used by the Swallow Brewery to dry hops. To do this they spread them out in the conical roof, and lit a fire beneath. The hops were stored in the annexe on the left. For a few years from 1938 it was a laundry and a scout hut.

The Old Malthouse, 1989. In 1978 a purchaser commissioned Neil Holland, a local architect, to convert it into a private dwelling house. The result is a home of unusual character. The former hearth on the ground floor is now the living room, and the conical roof above, a study.

SOURCES AND BIBLIOGRAPHY

For the old pictures:
Local Studies Library, Worthing.
Arundel Museum and Heritage Centre.
Joss Davis.
West Sussex Record Office.
Worthing Museum.

For much of the information:
Arundel Museum and Heritage Centre.
Eustace, *Arundel Borough and Castle*.
Allison, Francis D., *The Little Town of Arundel*.
Francis, *Ancient Arundel*.
Dunlop, R.O., *Ancient Arundel*.
Wright, J.C., *Arundel, A Medieval Town*.
Sussex County Magazine.
Sussex Life.
West Sussex Gazette.
Evening Argus.
Miscellaneous cuttings.